Published by Simon Nevill Publications
5 Novak Court, Hamilton Hill, Perth
Western Australia 6163
Email: snpub@bigpond.net.au

National Library of Australia Cataloguing-in-Publication data
Author: **Nevill**. Simon
Title: **Panoramic Journey through Western Australia**
ISBN 9780980348163
Panoramic photographs of Western Australia
Dewey Number: 994.1

Design concepts: **Simon J. Nevill**
Book design: **Sean McKay, FORGE**CREATIVE
Printed in China

PANORAMIC JOURNEY

through

CONTENTS

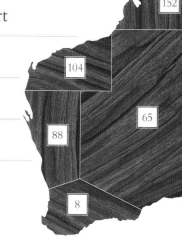

◄ *Previous page*   Rocks at Jorndee Inlet

◄ *This page*   Herrison Cove near Karratha

➡ *Following page*   Stirling Ranges

The map and regions above are purely schematic and do not adhere to any true geographical or botanical zoning.

INTRODUCTION

I have been fortunate enough to have travelled to nearly every corner of this vast state. Many times going where few people go. It has allowed me to get to know those very special places that have had a lasting impact on me. Over the last few years I have written several books related to the natural history world and guess in many ways I would consider myself a naturalist first and a photographer second. However, over the last two years something inside me felt the need to show the beauty of this state that I so regularly travel through. I wanted the reader to see not only the better known locations, but also those distant areas where they may not have been and to share the real beauty and feelings of those areas.

The majority of the photographs shown here are not intended to be works of great artistic merit, but simply to reflect the diversity of Western Australia. More like a celebration of the state. Taking landscape photographs may seem an easy task to do but it can require a lot of planning and discipline. I may see the day before, a location that has potential for what I hope will become a good photograph, so I will park the rig nearby, set up camp and wait for the following new day to arrive. The alarm is often set one hour before the sun has even risen. Off one goes, with head torch to guide me in the half light. Camera belt loaded and tripod over my shoulder and up the rocky mountain slope I climb. I get to the ridge top and look across a vast wilderness with the glow of the sky from a new dawning sun in the distance. Regardless of even taking the photograph, I am in that special place of respect and awe at the beauty and peace that surrounds me. That wonderful half light that envelops you, where the eye can absorb all light, as the talented photographer Peter Jarver, who sadly died far too young, would call 'Wild light'. These are the lengths one goes to, to capture those magic moments.

I have written some selective text to pass on small stories that may interest the reader and give more meaning to some of the locations. I hope that these photographs give you the same pleasure as I had when taking them, I also hope you might be spurred on to visiting some of these magnificent areas of our great state.

SOUTH WEST

This section of our photographic journey will take us south from Perth through the Margaret River and Walpole region, and all the way along the southern coast to the crystal blue waters of Esperance and Cape Arid. Then we head away from the coast, taking a brief look at the Stirling Range with its diverse flora of over 1,600 species of plant life and to a small, but precious reserve known as Dryandra Woodland located between the towns of Narrogin and Williams. Finally, a look at one of the many granite outcrops that are scattered throughout the Wheatbelt region.

Although the world of Ornithology (study of birds), is my main area of expertise, the south west, would not be noted as having a high number of bird species. That is the realm of the wet tropics of the world. However, what does occur here in vast numbers is its flora. In world terms, the flora diversity of the South West Botanic Zone is second only to South Africa. There are nearly 8,000 species of plant life here and 13,000 throughout the state. Simply staggering numbers.

To walk amongst what a botanist would call 'Kwongan Heath', in the Wheatbelt in spring, is an experience that visitors find absolutely astounding and many of those in busy lives do not appreciate the spectacular diversity.

All of the photographs in this section lie within the cultural boundaries of the Noongar people, the original custodians of this land. Many newly arrived settlers have little knowledge of the Noongar people, which is sad, as it is one of the largest indigenous cultural blocs to occur in Australia, comprising of 14 distinct clans. They lived in distinct habitat areas. The thick wetter jarrah forests supported several groups including the Ganeang, Whadjuk, Wilman, Binjareb and Balardong. Where as the dryer mallee regions of the outer Wheatbelt were the home of the Koreng, Wilman, and Wudjari. I don't mention this to be politically correct, but more to the point, when you traverse and see the beauty and diversity of this country, you will appreciate that it has supported its original occupants for thousands of years. When I stand on top of a granite outcrop, I really feel a connection with these people, I guess it's the 'bush man' in me.

← This page Mt Frankland near Walpole
→ Following page Hamersley Inlet, Fitzgerald National Park

PERTH

The population of Perth is growing fast and has now reached 1.7 million. Although relatively low compared to many cities in the rest of the world, it is however, quite disproportionate to the rest of the state. The city of Mandurah, south of Perth has a population of 84,000 at the most and the remainder of the state has a population of just 600,000 people.

Yes, Perth is a relatively large city but the area of Western Australia is more than half the size of the USA. That's big and its population small. That allows one the opportunity to get to areas where few people travel and often it's not far from Perth. All of the photographs shown in the south west section can be reached in a day. Agreed, Cape Arid would be a long days drive, but possible.

To some, the isolation of Perth from other cities is a detrimental thing, and to others, they love the fact that the nearest city with a million people, is over 2,000 km away.

Perth's western beaches are beautiful, there are few cities in the world that can boast an almost unbroken line of 50 km of white sandy beaches. When the big heat hits the city in mid summer, it is a saviour to many who congregate in their hundreds on the more popular locations. Fremantle is one of the few remaining colonial ports in the world that still retains a high percentage of the original colonial buildings of the mid to late 1800's. The majority are well preserved and maintained with heritage listings on all of them. Combine viewing these wonderful old buildings with a coffee and good conversations on the 'Cappuccino Strip', and you have the makings of a very pleasant day. I could have shown more photographs of Perth, but my heart is really in the country, and that's where I wish to take the reader on this photographic journey through this vast state.

◄ *Fremantle at night*

Perth Skyline

Original cottages at Thomson Bay, Rottnest Island.

Rottnest is such a peaceful place out of the busy summer season and many people come to escape the hustle and bustle of Perth. It is not so long ago in the geological time scale, that this peaceful island was attached to the mainland. We know that aboriginal artefacts have been found dating back to 6,500 years ago and longer when the island was connected to the mainland. It has had a chequered history. The first Europeans to sight the island were the Dutch. The first recordings being made by Frederick de Houtman, but it was the fellow Dutchman Willem de Vlamingh who named it "Rattenest", after the marsupial found on the island, the Quokka. The

first Europeans to settle on the island were Robert Thompson and his family. They gathered salt from the salt lakes and exported it to the mainland. It has sad memories for the Noongars, as there were approximately 3,600 Indigenous men and boys imprisoned here in the mid to late 1800's and many are buried on the island. They called the prison a 'Refractory for Savages'.

Since those sad days, the island has developed into a popular tourist destination and becomes incredibly busy in the summer months. Many of us love coming here in late April and May when the island is quieter and the weather still pleasant.

War Memorial, Kings Park, Perth.

Wars are terrible things, we see it in the past and we see it now. It often begs the question what is a "just war", almost an unanswerable question. What we do know is that in some wars if our forbears had not defended the right to have freedom and peace, many of us would not be standing here today. The First Word War saw the loss of over 60,000 Australian troops and a further 156,000 were either wounded, gassed or taken prisoner. The first battalions went to the Middle East to fight the Ottoman Empire and most know what happened at Anzac Cove, where the death toll was horrendous. If it was not for a well planned deception operation where hundreds of troops were evacuated, the death toll would have been even worse.

The Second World War saw nearly 40,000 Australian troops loose their lives and in Vietnam 521 troops died and 3,000 were wounded.

When I'm driving say, in the Wheatbelt and come to a small town, I'll often stop and walk over to their war memorial and read the names of the many lives lost, so many, so young. I think of what it would mean to these small towns where so many women were left to pick up the pieces. 'Lest we forget', is a powerful reminder to some of us.

Artwork Cottesloe Beach

Every year a wonderful event is held in Perth on the Cottesloe foreshore called 'Sculptures by the Sea'. It was the dream of founding director David Handley. While he was in the town of Klatovy in Bohemia, he went with friends to view a sculpture park set amongst 13th century ruins. There the seed was sown and while back in Sydney, he approached a receptive local council as well as sculptors to hold an event on one of the foreshores. There the dream became reality and later the concept was brought to Perth. David wanted the community to mingle and appreciate works of art in a free and relaxed environment. I think he has achieved that dream very well.

Pictured: 'Fissures' by the sculptor Tony Davis

Queen Mary departing Fremantle

Breakwater Hotel, Hillarys

'Cappucino Strip' Fremantle

Karri Forrest

The Karri tree is a magnificent species of eucalypt and is one of the tallest trees in the world, reaching heights of 90m (300 ft). Its Latin name is '*Eucalyptus diversicolor*' meaning 'separate colours', which refers to the top of the leaf being darker than the underside. The word Karri comes from the Noongar name for the tree. The Karri can be found in the far west near Augusta, in the east as far as the Porongorup Range and also the Mt Manypeaks area. Alongside these giant trees grow some other more restricted eucalypts, namely Red Tingle (*E. guilfoylei*), Yellow Tingle (*E. jacksonii*) and the most restricted distribution is Rates Tingle (*E, brevistylis*). The buttress of the Red Tingle can be several meters wide far larger than those of Karri trees.

Swarbrick art installation, Walpole.

Swarbrick is an art installation set amongst tall Karri trees and is a wonderful project that DEC instigated with the artists Lorena Grant and Alan Clarke. The picture above shows the 'wall of words', which basically describes the perceptions and feelings that one can have for the forest environment and stimulates one to reflect on ones own feelings about the forests. There is a short pathway into the forest where the artists have set five more art works that are suspended from the surrounding eucalypts. Oh! for more of this type of art work. The installation is just 8 km north of Walpole on the Mt Frankland Road.

Fernhook Falls north east of Walpole

➡ *Following page*
Elephant Rocks west of Walpole. These are some of the largest granite boulders to be seen along the entire south west coast.

The sun sets across Green Pool, which lies at the eastern end of Mazzoletti Beach. One of the few safe beaches to swim at on the southern coast as it is well protected by a rocky barrier 300 meters off the coast hence the calm sea.

Waychinicup is a magical place to visit. I have friends who make a regular pilgrimage there to spend quality time for a week or so. Other friends I knew would take a Christmas cake every year to the hermit who lived in shack at the inlet. Now, only the coloured tiles of his walkway path remain as reminders of his past life. Illustrated here are birds that are endemic to Western Australia and found here at Waychinicup. Two of the birds, the Western Whipbird (on the cut off branch) and the Western Bristlebird (the all brown coloured bird) are extremely elusive and not easy to see but their calls, once known, make them easier to find. The stunning little Red-winged Fairywren can be found in the damper regions of the south west. From just north of Perth to east of Waychinicup and often found in the gardens of homes along the southern coast.

◂ Waychinicup Inlet 40 km east of Albany

When Mathew Flinders sailed along the southern coastline, he named the three prominent quartzite hills, now located in the Fitzgerald River National Park. East, Mid and West Mt Barren, alluding to the fact that no tall eucalypts could be seen on the hills but if he had taken the time to walk this country he would be spell-bound at the diversity of plant life and would certainly not call them 'Barren'. The botanist William Baxter, was astounded by the diversity of flora, way back in 1830. He was so excited with the multi coloured leaves of the plant known as Royal Hakea (*H. victoria* in honour of Queen Victoria), that he rode back on his horse to Albany, some 180 km through some of the thickest impenetrable scrub with his precious sample, to show his friends, Only to find that when he finally got to Albany, all the leaves had dried out and turned a dull brown. If one has a bent towards the natural history world, one would not know where to begin describing this rich flora wonderland. The Fitzgerald River National Park has over 1,900 species of plant life, the largest of range of any park in Western Australia. The quantity of banksias alone, will astound the visitor. If you visit Point Anne in the park in August, you should see the mighty Humpback Whales with their young calves, very close to the beach. It's a wonderful sight set overlooking a beautiful 6 km long white sandy beach.

Early dawn at Stokes Inlet half way between Ravensthorpe and Esperance

Early dawn at Stokes Inlet half way between Ravensthorpe and Esperance

Blue Haven Beach, Esperance.

I have travelled many times to Queensland, admiring their wonderful beaches but many people are not aware of the wonderful clear blue colours of the ocean along the Esperance coast, particularly when it is set against the pure white sands. No wonder this beach is called 'Blue Haven'.

Twilight Bay, Esperance.

The town of Esperance was named after one of the French vessels 'L'Esperance', Commanded by Captain Bruni D'Entrecasteaaux, who sailed the Southern Ocean in 1792. Mathew Flinders came later, charting the islands of the Recherche Archipelago.

A lone salt bleached log at Hamersley inlet taken after the sun has set

This beautiful tranquil bay would have become the most joyous place to be for the intrepid explorer Edward John Eyre and his fellow Aboriginal traveller, Wylie. For it was here on the 2nd of June 1840 that they miraculously came across the whaling vessel the 'Mississippi', under the command of the English master Captain Rossiter.

Lack of water had plagued the 2,000 km journey that Eyre and Wylie made from Adelaide, at last they had plentiful water and food to assist them on their journey to Albany.

On this horrendous journey Eyre's companion, overseer John Baxter was murdered by the two accompanying Aborigines Joey and Yarry. Eyre felt very much alone and worried that Wylie may not be reliable. But he turned out to be the most loyal companion, staying with Eyre all the way to Albany. Wylie remained with his people in the Albany region and was rewarded with a pension. Eyre went on to become Lieutenant Governor of New Zealand. Eyre still held a great respect for Wylie and while in New Zealand sent him a double barrelled shot gun knowing that he was a keen hunter. When the Western Australian Government refused to honour a commitment to supply Wylie with a monthly ration of flour and tobacco, it was Eyre who intervened. When you travel through the most strenuous conditions with a fellow traveller you develop a close respect. Eyre must have, over the years developed a respect for the Aboriginal people as he was given the post of 'Protector of Aborigines' near Blanchetown, South Australia.

Lucky Bay, Cape Le Grand National Park.

Hellfire Bay, Cape Le Grand National Park.

Thistle Cove, Cape Le Grand National Park.

My life can be hectic, travelling hundreds of kilometres, I will usually only stop overnight in each place, planning shots in the evening and morning. Occasionally an area just grabs me and while in Cape Arid National Park, I saw the small '4WD only', sign to a beach, always tempting for me. I turned off and found three secluded camping bays set amongst the tall Showy Banksia's (*Banksia speciosa*). I parked the rig and took a narrow walking track over the sand dune. Below me was a beautiful bay and then just to my right was the inlet for Jorndee Creek. I was in heaven! I stayed two nights, for me a rare thing when on the move. I would have taken over 20 panoramas while at that location, such was the potential for good shots. I'll be back that's for sure.

← *Jorndee Creek, Cape Arid national Park.*
→ *Following page Dawn at Yokinup Bay, Cape Arid National Park.*

Coastal Granite

Much of the overlaying sands have long been washed away, exposing the southern boundary of the ancient granite rocks of the massive Yilgarn Craton, which covers an area 65,000 sq.km. These ancient hard rocks have not been covered by seas since they were uplifted 3000 million years ago. I find the granite and the dolerite volcanic rocks of the southern coastline draw me like a magnet and I wish I had another life, to know more about the forces of nature that have developed these amazing land forms. My camera certainly is drawn to them.

Coastal Granite

THE STIRLING RANGE

The Stirling Range is another flora wonderland. The Range has a flora species list of over 1,600, only second to the Fitzgerald River National Park. Many species can only be found on the higher slopes of the mountains. The mountain bells of the Darwinia group are of particular interest, they are often restricted to a few peaks with many growing at the very highest levels of the range. The quartz rich, but mineral deficient soils of the lower slopes support a wealth of wildflowers. In the clay and quartz soils of the Wandoo woodland, the variety of orchids will astound you in spring. The staff at the privately owned Stirling Range Retreat located close to Bluff Knoll can show you many species and to see the Queen of Sheba orchid (*Thelymitra variegata - pictured page 59*) in mid August to early September is a real bonus.

◀ On top of Bluff Knoll

In these few square meters shown in the photograph above on Baby Barnet Hill in the Stirling Range, there may be as many 30 species of flowering plant.

◄ *The alpine flora high up on Bluff Knoll*

➔ *Following page Baladgie Rock, North Eastern Wheatbelt.*

This photograph summarises many things for me. Farms are getting bigger to make them more viable, buildings and homesteads are left abandoned, with the original occupants long gone. At present I am in the middle of a huge book on the Wheatbelt writing about it's past and present. I have talked to farmers struggling and have interviewed the wealthiest farmers in the Wheatbelt. One man comes to mind who is so unpretentious, he stands in bare feet, hardened by a life of hard toil, as he chats to me below huge grain silos costing 12 million. These people are for the most part, some of the finest people you could wish to meet. Their support for their fellow farmers knows no bounds and I am often humbled by their kindness when I visit them. Alas, the book has become such a big project, I have had to put it on hold as I need to eat and that book will have to stay in the wings for a while but it will be completed.

Dryandra Woodland Reserve

Many of my friends know that this small reserve in the Wheatbelt, between Williams and Narrogin holds a special place for me. It is the bolthole I return to when the city is getting me down. Here in this remnant woodland, some of our few remaining rare mammals manage to survive. In part, it is thanks to the dedicated work of DEC scientists and volunteers who have helped save some species from the brink of extinction. One such species is the Numbat shown above. Many of you will know about this animal, although many may not realize that this is Western Australia's fauna emblem. In the 1980's the population was estimated to be only 300 individuals. This decline was attributed to loss of habitat through land clearing, combined with the devastating introduction of the European Fox in the early 1900's.

The Numbat is the only marsupial to be solely diurnal (out during the day). It can be a slack little creature, not venturing out of its log hollow retreat until mid morning, if the temperatures are not of its liking. They feed exclusively on subterranean termites using their 100 mm long tongue.

They raise their young mostly in fallen hollow tree trunks, bringing leaf and bark litter to build their nest. Young are born during mid summer and leave their nest hollow in September and by October they will be venturing further from their retreat with their mother and then finally disperse in late November to early December.

To know these little creatures are still alive and well is wonderful, although their populations are still in the balance. The flora in the Kwongan heath of Dryandra Reserve is very rich, as the photograph shows and the reserve holds over 800 species of plant life. You can stay in the old timber woodcutters cottages for a small fee. If you have not been then think about a bush experience here in spring.

GOLDFIELDS & DESERT

The Goldfields has a character all of its own. You can see it etched in its early history. When Arthur Bayley registered a claim at Fly Flat in Coolgardie in 1892, the 'Goldrush' had commenced. A year later when the Irishmen Patrick Hannan, Tom Flanagan and Daniel Shea were forced to camp due to one of their horses loosing a shoe at Mt Charlotte, it was to turn out to be the most fortunate mishap, for over the next two days they found over 100 ounces of alluvial gold. That cemented the 'Goldrush' and within a few years Coolgardie had 30,000 people living under tin and canvas. Today, there are still 6th generation miners working the huge open pit on the Golden Mile in Kalgoorlie. Our photographic journey here takes us from the stony Goldfields, way out to country that is very close to my heart, the desert regions. This is a vast area covering half of Western Australia. It can be uncompromising and if you are ill equipped to enter these remote areas it may be your demise. There were some amazing exploits across these vast spinifex clad sand dune deserts. The list is long, John and Alexander Forrest, Peter Warburton, David Carnegie, Ernest Giles, Frank Hann, Alfred Canning, Samuel Talbot, William Everard, Francis Gregory and many more. Many of these expeditions had the objective of finding inland waters or better pastoral country. What they did find were miles and miles of desert sand dunes and certainly no large bodies of permanent water. They often came close to death in their exploits. First, they used horses to explore and found these poor creatures totally inadequate for this form of travel and camels became by far the best solution. Some were kind to the indigenous inhabitants, some were certainly not. The one man that has made desert exploration far more accessible for 4WD vehicles was the amazing Len Beadell, surveyor, roadbuilder extraordinaire and amazing character, who himself came close to death in the deserts. He developed numerous tracks that traversed much of central Australia including the Anne Beadell Highway, The Connie Sue, The Gunbarrel, The Gary Highway and The Gary Junction Road. The photographs included here are often taken far from the nearest civilization and I hope they impart the joy that I get from being alone in some very special places.

Giles Breakaway on the Laverton-Warburton Road in the Victoria Desert

65

Sunrise on Lake Ballard

The original occupants of Wanjarri Station have long gone. The photograph reminds us of a sheep station's past and the years of hard work and toil in establishing a property and trying to make it viable.

It has bred a hardy people. When the truck breaks down, you don't panic
but light up the fire, boil the billy and then take your time to fix it.

The setting sun breaks through the storm clouds brightening up the mottled bark of my favourite eucalypt, the Marble Gum (*Eucalyptus gongylocarpa*). These lovely desert eucalypts have a range from east of Sandstone all the way across to Lake Amadeus in the Northern Territory. Marble Gums, like many eucalypts, flower in midsummer providing nectar to help see the desert honeyeaters through the summer months. We often think that the desert is a merciless period in the middle of summer and most of the time it is, but it is often the time when cyclonic storms can drop several inches of rain across these spinifex plains. Surprisingly, many bird species will breed right through this time, for even though the temperatures can be hot, the dry yellow Spinifex turns lush green and the insect life proliferates. Insects are the main source of protein for the dry country birds like Striated Grassrwens and Rufous-crowned Emuwrens, as well as the diminutive nocturnal marsupials like the Hairy-footed Dunnart, Kultarr and Mulgara.

Lorna Glen Station now forms part of the Gascoyne-Murchison Strategy Plan. The objective of this project is to restore some former pastoral leases to their original natural state. or as close as possible and to be viable by the year 2020. Scientists, volunteers and conservation experts as well as the traditional custodians, the 'Martuwa', have been working on this long term project now for at least 10 years. Murdoch University and the Perth Zoo have also assisted on various projects, so it has become a very valuable research reserve for several organizations working closely with DEC. As yet, access is restricted to scientists and volunteers but the public will one day be able to visit when the reserve is well established and there are adequate facilities.

The eastern end of the Schwerin Mural Crescent close to the Northern Territory border

I'm standing close to where the explorer Ernest Giles and his trusted offsider William Henry Tietkins passed by in mid January 1874. I quote from his writings "I called this the Pass of the Abencerrages, that is to say, the Children of the Saddle". Reading his travels in 'Australia Twice Traversed', you realize how well read Giles was, albeit, a romantic, for he was forever quoting the early classical scholars. Travelling in the deserts in mid summer was never a good plan and that's what he did on this particular trip. They were lucky here, as throughout most of the central ranges there are some permanent water holes and that saved him and his horses many times but the agonies that were to follow were unimaginable. It was to lead to the death of young Gibson who eventually became lost in what we now call the Gibson Desert. Taking horses was never

a good plan and they were constantly losing them and having to track them down. Their need for water every 3-4 days at the very least, took its toll on the expedition as many horses died. Giles, on his final expeditions had learned to take camels and that made his travels a far easier task as they can endure going without water for up to 18 days which is an incredible feat. Giles was an amazing adventurer, surviving many attacks by indigenous groups protecting their water holes and country. He came close to dieing of thirst several times, especially when looking for young Gibson. Giles ended his days as a clerk in wardens office in Coolgardie, eventually dieing of pneumonia and sadly obscurity. A sad ending to someone who had done so much to map the desert regions of this country.

Hann Pass in the Blackstone Range east of Warburton

I talked to an elderly lady for long while at Papulankutja (Blackstone) and it turned out that she was born alongside a small water hole in the pass you can see ahead, that breaks through the ranges. The pass was named after the explorer Frank Hann, who is not so well known as many of the other explorers, which is a pity as he surveyed so much of Western Australia and named an incredible number of landmarks. All can be read in his very detailed diaries. Luckily there is a major park in the south west named in his honour, Frank Hann National Park where he surveyed much of the country.

The sun sets on Mt Clianthus in the Blackstone Range

The wild light of twilight looking east from Mt Fanny towards Mt Daisy Bates in the far distance

Daisy Bates, what a lady. Yes, she was eccentric and often held very controversial views on indigenous culture and history, but sometimes, I say, it's better at least to roll up your sleeves and do something rather than stand on the sidelines advising but doing nothing - she did a lot of 'doing' albeit sometimes misguided.

Few people know that she was actually married to the bushman, poet and horseman, Breaker Morant. That marriage did not last and the subsequent one either, although she had a boy from the second marriage but sadly in later life he would have nothing to do with his mother. After her disenchantment with marriage, the Irish immigrant returned to England and while there she became a journalist. On reading in 'The Times', an article on the mistreatment of Aborigines in Western Australia, she applied to them to write articles on the subject if she could return to Australia. The 'Times', accepted her offer. For the next 35 years she worked with various indigenous groups. They called her 'Kabbarli', meaning white grandmother. Later she was appointed 'Travelling Protector of Aborigines', in Western Australia. Her final years were spent with communities in South Australia, eventually returning to Adelaide as her health was deteriorating and it is where she is now buried.

A complex lady, but she did so much to fight for the protection of indigenous people, so much so that it is reported she carried a pistol in her side bag to protect the indigenous ladies if whites accosted them. She was certainly outside the box.

After light on Mt Fanny on the Mulga Park Road north of Irrunytju (Wingellina)

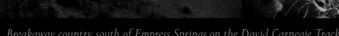

Breakaway country south of Empress Springs on the David Carnegie Track

Below this breakaway I found several large caves. In one there were three stones, one was a grinding stone and alongside a large quartz rock. There were no large quartz in the vicinity and on examining it, I realized it was used for chipping flakes for cutting tools or spear heads. Needless to say, they were returned to where I had found them. Evidence of bye gone days of the indigenous peoples presence and knowing the harsh environment I am standing in, brings it home how tenacious and resilient these central desert people are. This region overlaps with the two language groups, the Nyanganyatjara and Nyaanyatjarra. The cave you see here with the steel ladder is known as Empress Springs. It was named by David Wynford Carnegie although in his diary he called it Empress Soak after Queen Victoria. Carnegie was lead to the water hole by an Aborigine who initially lead them far from the springs to a dried up water hole some five hours walking distance away. He was hoping to escape and not show them the precious waterhole but the party knew what he had done and seeing their anger he eventually led them to Empress Springs. One must understand why they were so reluctant to show these life saving waters. Long before whites had explored the central deserts, tales of the Europeans presence in the Goldfields taking the permanent water holes must have filtered through from other clan groups. Clans communicated with others outside of their 'skin group', this was how marriages were arranged.

Camping near Breaden Bluff and Empress Springs. Time to reflect and enjoy a desert sunset, knowing I'm the only person here in this remote part of the northern Victoria Desert.

Imagine the loss of water at Empress Springs after Carnegies visit. The group was made up of five men including the wonderful guide Warri and a large team of camels. They had been without water for 13 days and when they had set out from their last watering point, they had taken 66 gallons to be shared between the five men, remembering that the camels would be given no water. When they finally got to Empress Springs they had just one gallon left. What amazes me when reading Carnegies book 'Spinifex and Sand', where he detailed his epic journey from the Goldfields through the deserts to Halls Creek and all the way back again, was the fact that when he got to Halls Creek after experiencing the most gruelling and often near fatal journey,

(it was fatal for poor Stansmore, he accidentally shot himself falling on his rifle), Carnegie gave his offsiders three choices for their return journey to Perth. One, they could return to Perth via the well worn coastal tracks through the stations like De Gray Station. Two, they could travel by boat from Wyndam to Perth or thirdly, return through the central deserts and do it all over again. Well, return through the deserts they did! Breaden, Carnegies main offsider said "Well I've been in the bush all my life but you're the only man that I'd let do as he likes and follow him, in country like this". Such was the camaraderie and respect for this heroic explorer.

A lone rocky knoll surrounded by endless spinifex plains and sand dunes east of Lake Auld near the Canning Stock Route in the Great Sandy Desert

→ *Following page* *Breaden Hills at sunset*

That wonderful half light as the sunsets on the Breaden Hills named by the explorer David Carnegie after his main offsider, big Joe Breaden, who he considered to be an absolute gentleman. They lie at the northern end of the Canning Stock Route and are part of the Southesk Tablelands, also named by Carnegie after his father James Carnegie, the ninth Earl of Southesk. David was seen as the black sheep of the family as he chose to wander the remote parts of Australia rather than spend time in his regal home in Scotland. Here in these hills they found precious water and at Godfrey's Tank (Wajanturumanu), enough for the men and camels. It has a large capacity but some years it may be dry and even though Breaden Pool (Wajanturumanu) is smaller, I have found over the years it can hold water longer. When Alfred Canning on his 1906 exploration establishing the Canning Stock Route visited this area, both water holes were dry as it was an exceptionally dry year.

David Carnegie encountered the local indigenous people here in these hills, the males having bunched up hair with Emu feathers as plumes. They were most probably Tjurabalan or Mindibungu people whose land borders this region and their Walmalarri language is still spoken as the first language around Lake Gregory (Paruku). Many of the older generation living today were stockman helping to take stock down the Canning or working on the local stations.

Carnegie was tough sometimes on indigenous people when he travelled through the harshest parts of the desert, forcing them to show him where water could be found when he desperately needed it, although no where near as bad as the earlier explorer Warburton who's diaries Carnegie took on his travels. In these enlightened times things would be done differently but Carnegie was basically a good man in fact when he made his two desert explorations he was only in his mid twenties. With one group of indigenous people he spent hours with his limited medicines, attending to swollen eyes of children and adults alike. His explorations were in the end his undoing as he was killed by a poison dart, while exploring in Africa, dieing at the young age of 29.

The Breaden Hills glow as I take my shot from the Canning Stock Route track near the turn off to Well 48. The Canning Stock Route is well known to many. Alfred Wernam Canning in 1906 under the direction of the Surveyor General was given the task of establishing a stock route from Wiluna to Halls Creek. The Goldfields population was growing so fast and the plan was to bring cattle down to feed this new expanding populous. It was a massive task that took thirteen months to complete and when that was done, Canning followed the construction crew sinking the fifty plus wells that took a further two years from March 1908 till March 1910. It was an incredible feat and Canning himself was a tenacious and resilient man. He had already surveyed the longest vermin fence in the world, the Rabbit Proof Fence which is nearly 2,000 kms long.

His physical strength to endure hardship was amazing. He once, while trying to reach the small telegraph station at Wallal Station on Eighty Mile Beach, walked the last 70 kms to reach it after his camel could go no further. He sent a brief telegram and then returned to his desert camp in the Great Sandy Desert walking in total some 150 kms in three and half days, an amazing feat. In 1929, when he was 69 years of age, he was approached to repair and open up his original wells laid in 1908 to 1910 as they had run into disrepair. His assistants who worked on each well reported how he would walk to each well, on average 25 kms apart, opening up the track as a guide for his party to follow. Some feat at 69, he died only 7 years later and is buried in Karrakatta Cemetery.

MID WEST

The **Mid West region** is noted for its amazing displays of everlasting wildflowers providing good winter rains have fallen. This land is sheep station country where breakaways, granite outcrops and occasional uplifted mountain ranges break the undulating hills covered mostly in mulga woodland. There are a few large rivers that cut through this region, the main ones being the Gascoyne in the north, Murchison in the middle and to a lesser degree, the Greenough River in the south. Our photographic journey starts in the unique Benedictine town of New Norcia and then wanders through the midwest to the Cape Range in the north. The station country has taken a pounding in the last few years with extensive droughts throughout the region. Many pastoralists have had to sell and leave their properties, however, most keep going and good rains will come like they have this year, in the upper Murchison and Gascoyne region.

The Monastery entrance at New Norcia

New Norcia is a Spanish Roman Catholic Mission town located on the Victoria Plains about 130 km north of Perth. It is certainly unique, as it is the only monastic town in Australia. When one visits the small town, the neo classical Spanish architecture comes as a real surprise but there is a sense of peace here, the original concept for the mission was the so called 'Civilization and Christenizing of the Aborigines'. The foundation stone was laid in 1847. It was inaugurated in 1848 by Bishop Rosendo Salvado, a Spanish Benedictine monk. He named it New Norcia, which was the birthplace of St Benedict in Italy. Salvado was born in the village of Tui, Galicia, Spain in 1814. He was forced to leave his region in Spain due to the anti-catholic governments restrictions under Isabella II of Spain, who closed many monasteries down and also secularised monks. After he was ordained, Salvado left for Australia to set up the mission in New Norcia. The early years were extremely hard for the small band of Monks and Salvado returned to Spain to raise funds for the mission. In 1853 he returned with some monks who were to go to various missions throughout Australia. but he returned to New Norcia. Over the years more European settlers were moving to this area and the emphasis and direction of the mission changed to supporting the white population. In 1867 Salvado was given the status of 'Lord Abbot' and the mission became an independent Abbey. He died while on a journey to Rome, however his body was returned to Australia and one can see the head stone at the New Norcia Cemetery.

The Benedictine Community owns 30,000 acres of land that surrounds the community. Two huge schools remain today, one was the boys school, St Lidephonsus and the other the girls, St Gertrude's. There were also two schools for indigenous children, St Mary's for the boys and St Joseph's for the girls. They no longer are used as schools now but are used for various functions as well as accommodation for groups. The present Abbot is John Herbert appointed in 2009. The Benedictine Monks practice a rigid program of prayer, I should know, I went myself, even though I follow no given faith. I was staying at the guesthouse to take time from a busy schedule. While there, I read their program for Morning Prayer times and it was certainly demanding. There were three prayer gatherings in their own chapel before breakfast. If memory serves me, the first was at 5.00am then 6.00am and finally at 7.00am. I thought if they could do this 365 days of the year then I at least could try for one day in the year and I did. You don't join them in song but sit quietly on the side benches. I was the only person besides the small band of monks for the first two sessions. It was a wonderful atmosphere for me, to hear these monks singing in such a peaceful place. It was like going back in time, a world far removed from the pressures of city life.

In the late 1800's the Monks from New Norcia shepherded their sheep on the station pictured to the right. The old sheep pens still remain as well as the original old homestead still in use today.

Dawn on the top of Mt Singleton, Ninghan Station south of Paynes Find.

The Kennedy Range is an uplifted mass of sandstone that has over time eroded away on the eastern face. To the west is the Carnarvon Basin which was once a shallow ocean basin laying on the edge of the main Australian continent. Over millions of years the sediments on the sea floor were compressed to form layers of shale and sandstone. With the movement of the continents, the sandstone rocks were thrust upwards to form a huge plateaux. Now there is a continuous mesa scarp running 70 km long from north to south. The cliff faces you see rise up 100 m from the surrounding plains. Within the range can be found marine fossils and also early plant life. A wonderfully preserved Banksia cone was found in the range showing that the proteacea family grew here many thousands of years ago.

Everlastings litter the understorey below the acacia woodland on the top of Coalseam Gorge, inland from Geraldton. Coalseam National Park is a very small park surrounded by farming country and you come upon it almost by surprise after driving for miles through wheat fields. Through the centre of the park runs the Irwin River, which has cut a deep gorge through the sandstone and shale. There are numerous fossils in the lower gorge. If the Mulga country north of Mullewa has been experiencing severe drought and there are not reasonable displays of everlastings, you can always visit Coalseam, as there is a greater chance of seeing everlastings as it tends to receive a little more rain.

On top of a breakaway on the Woodleigh Road at sunset north of Murchison Settlement

Huge granite boulders on Wooleen Station

Wooleen is a wonderful station that one can stay at. It's a magnificent property for the naturalist as it has such a diverse habitat. There is a huge lake system, part of the flood plain of the Roderick River that flows into the Murchison in very wet years. When the lake is full, thousands of waterbirds descend on the lake. The fringing lush grasslands and samphire support large numbers of the stunning Orange Chat as well as hard to see birds like Inland Dotterel. One year when the Mulga was so green and the everlastings were everywhere I set up my hide to photograph certain nesting birds. I would estimate than in just 300 sq.m there would have been 10 - 20 nests, such was the density of breeding.

You can stay on the station in well appointed rammed earth chalets or camp close to the old homestead. There are also many other station properties in the Murchison and Gascoyne region where one can stay and I recommend it to those who have never experienced station life.

Carpets of Everlastings south of Overlander Road House in the northern Murchison region

During the summer the dry red stony soils of the Mid West look so barren and denuded. However, below the surface lay the dormant seeds of the Asteraceae family, one of the worlds largest families of flowering plants and second largest in Australia, we all know them as Daisies. If rains are plentiful in the winter months, these seeds will germinate and form carpets of everlastings that transform the once barren looking soils to a sea of vibrant colour. There are many differing species of daisy and depending on the type of habitat and location the hills will become covered in sheets of pink, yellow, purple or rose red everlastings.

Carpets of Splendid Everlastings (Rhodanthe chlorocephala) line the roadside verge of the Murchison Road north of Mullewa

Everlastings have stiff, papery bracts (the petals) circling around the central florets. They almost invariably are bright in colour and the petals have the attribute of retaining their bright colour even when the stem has dried or even cut, hence the name everlastings.

Everlastings were even exported to Europe in the late 18th century and it was not too long before growers were cultivating them and creating various hybrids with all sorts of flamboyant colours. When driving, say on the Great Northern Highway, the species past Wubin will differ from those just north of Paynes Find and as you progress north of Meekatharra they will change yet again, so one species will not be found all the way to the Pilbara, it will be several different kinds.

Western Bowerbird

These jagged cliffs are compressed marine sediments, now turned to rock laid down some 20 to 30 million years ago, when tropical seas covered much of the region. With the movements of the continents the ancient seabed was thrust upwards to form the Cape Range. Rains have carved their way through the gullies deepening and widening them overtime. In the rocky hills, a subspecies of the beautiful Western Bowerbird can be found with the male sporting a lilac neck collar that he inflates when courting at his bower. The male bowerbird plays no part in the nesting process, that is left to the female who raises the young and builds the nest. The male's work is confined to maintaining the bower, a complex avenue of twigs neatly woven together. He will lay white land snail shells or small white bleached bones, even glass or white quartz at the entrance to the avenue. Added to this he will place on top of the white objects, either

unripe green fruits of the Rock Fig (*Ficus platypoda*), or the fruits of the Northern Sandalwood (*Santalum lanceolatum*). The bright greens will stand out from the more prolific white stones and white land snail shells of which there will be far more, almost like a backdrop canvas of a painting. He will hiss and make gurgling and rasping calls from a high vantage point in a nearby tree. If he sees an interested female is attracted by his calls, he will drop down to the bower continuing the calls even more vigorously. If she then drops down to the bower, he will start strutting and performing a sideways dance, hopping from side to side while angling his head to one side, revealing a bright pink row of neck feathers like an extended fan. While doing this, he will enter the narrow avenue of vertical twigs. If she is happy with the structure of the bower and his performance she may walk through the bower inspecting it and if things are just right, she may present herself to the male and mating will occur, normally very close to the bower. The male is totally polygamous, mating with any female that is attracted to the bower. The whole performance is very complex but a wonderful sight to see, if you have the privilege to witness it.

Looking across the blue clear water of Shark Bay near Skipjack Point at the northern tip of Cape Peron in Francois Peron National Park

The park is named after the French naturalist Francois Peron who accompanied Nicholas Baudin on his 1801 expedition to 'New Holland' (Australia). Peron sadly, had lost an eye in battles while fighting in the revolutionary army in the late 1700's. He was a very keen naturalist and when he heard that Nicholas Baudin was planning a major expedition to the 'South Lands' or 'New Holland', he persuaded Baudin to allow him to come. It was the worst decision that Baudin could have made as they became enemies, subsequently writing reports after the expedition of the failings of the other. However, the expedition was extremely well equipped, far more than any of the British expeditions. For example, on Flinders expedition there was only one botanist, Robert Brown, who luckily did great work recording the plants of Australia. Baudin's party sailed on two ships, the Le Geographe and Le Naturaliste. It was one of the largest scientific teams ever sent to Australia, consisting of several botanists, anthropologists, natural history artists and even mineralogists. The art works done are some of the finest of all early pioneer expeditions. Many of the artists and naturalists never made the journey to Australia, due to arguments and misgivings about the journey and they disembarked on the French colonial islands of Mauritius. Of those scientists that did remain only 7 made it to New Holland, the rest sadly died of either dysentery or scurvy. One good thing that did come out of this terrible journey is that Peron made a life long friend in Charles Alexandre Lesueur. Both were very young men at the time. Peron however, was far more qualified in the natural sciences as Lesueur was commissioned as an artist only. Peron trained him in the natural sciences as well as the physical work of taxidermy and even how to trap for animals.

Both Peron and Lesueur and other members had collected the largest collection of natural history of any expedition to date, with over 100,000 specimens collected, an amazing feat.

When they returned to France in 1804, Peron wrote a journal titled 'Voyage de decouvertes aux Terres Australes', of which Lesueur did all the illustrations.

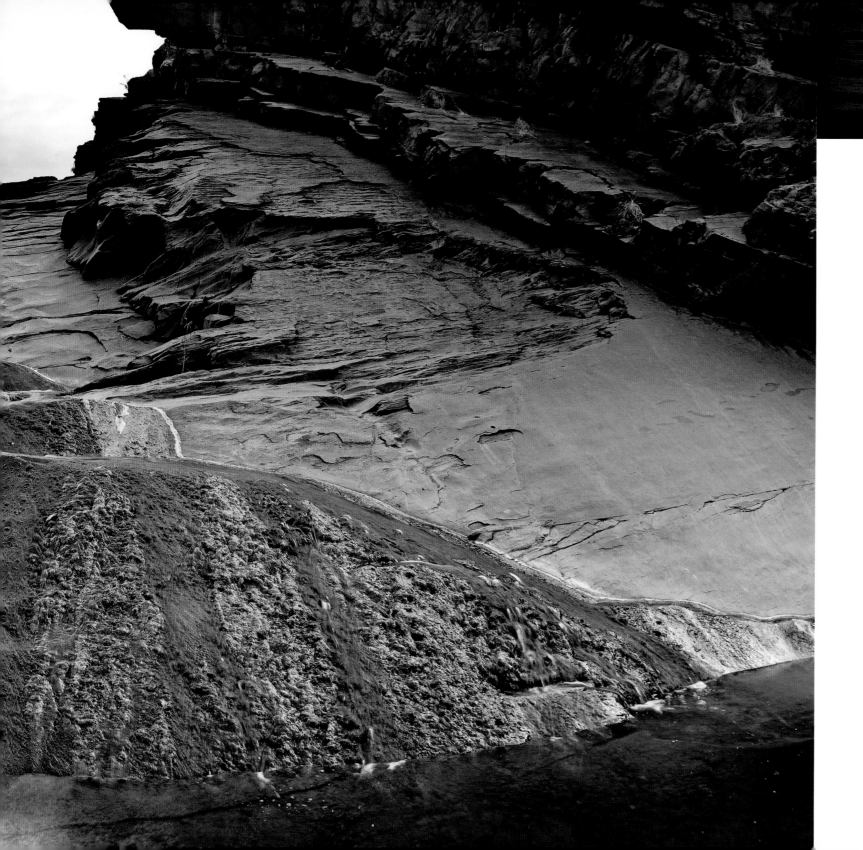

PILBARA

The photographic journey in the Pilbara region starts on the Burrup Peninsula. Here you can find the greatest concentration of rock engravings found anywhere in the world. We then head up into the Hamersley Range where so many deep gorges have cut through the banded ironstone, then a quick look north of Millstream to Python Pool. We continue on to the eastern side of the Pilbara to the jasper rocks at Marble Bar, then even further east to beautiful Carawine Gorge not far from the edge of the Great Sandy Desert.

The Pilbara is a geologist's dream. The rocks vary from being the oldest in Australia to young sedimentary rocks. At the core of the region is the spectacular Hamersley Range, part of the Pilbara Craton, geologically, a very stable region now joined to the far larger Yilgarn Craton to the south forming what is known as the 'Western Sheild'. Both the Yilgarn and Pilbara Craton were once separated and over time they came together causing immense pressure that uplifted the Hamersley Range we see today. The rocks in the Pilbara are even older than those in the Yilgarn and within the greater Pilbara region there is a multitude of rock types including banded ironstone, dolomite, siltstones, basalt, slates, clays, mudstones, chert, sandstone, limestone and more. The variety is so great that geologists from around the world gravitate to this area to study the evolution of these most ancient rocks. It is one area in Western Australia where you can see in just one location many forms of rock type. A classic example is Hamersley Gorge on the western side of the Hamersley Range.

The company Woodside Petroleum has a huge installation on the Burrup Peninsular producing vast quantities of LNG (liquefied natural gas). It is a contentious issue to many, as the plant lies right along side the largest collection of petroglyphs (rock engravings) in the world. I don't intend to bog myself down on this issue but focus on the art itself.

The calm waters at Herrison Cove on the Burrup Peninsula

It was in this small bay on the 13th of May 1861, that Frances Thomas Gregory and his party landed off the barque the 'Dolphin'. The objective of his travels was to find suitable areas to grow cotton. The Pilbara obviously would be the last place to grow cotton but what he did achieve was opening up the North West region for the pastoral industry.

Amongst the rocks I am standing on and those in the distance, are scattered scores of engravings.

Petroglyphs at Herrison Cove

Luckily, about 90% of the petroglyphs on Burrup Peninsula remain and they certainly need to be well protected. There are estimates of 200,000 to over a million engraved motifs on the peninsula. The engravings are etched into a type of fine grained granite known as granophyre, which consists of feldspar and quartz. The other granite here is gabbro which consists mostly of pyroxene, most engravings are on the granophyre rocks. The fine grains of the rock, although hard, allow intricate shapes to be carved. Most of the indigenous artwork in the Pilbara are petroglyphs, unlike the indigenous people of the Kimberley who solely use various colours of ochres to paint their motifs. The indigenous name for the Burrup is 'Murujuga' meaning 'hip bone sticking out' referring to the way the peninsula juts out into the Dampier Archipelago. Besides the engravings, there are standing stones and also near the beaches, middens which are piles of shells left after the contents were eaten. This area is the ancestral home of the Yabburara people but in 1868 there was a terrible massacre here known as 'Flying Foam Massacre'. Twenty six Yaburara people were killed. The numbers of Yaburara on the peninsular were never high, so the loss of so many people had a devastating effect on the population and they left the region.

On the eastern road side of Karigini National Park

The classic Pilbara scene, spinifex, red termite mounds and red rocks.

I have passed by this twisted old Migum (Eucalyptus leucophloia sub.sp. leucophloia) tree for over 25 years. It's older than me and will most probably outlast me too. Walking to the base of the tree, you realize the real tenacity of these gums that survive on such hard stony grounds.

Twilight near Hamersley Gorge in the western part of Karijini

Sunsets in the north of the state are invariably more spectacular than in the south

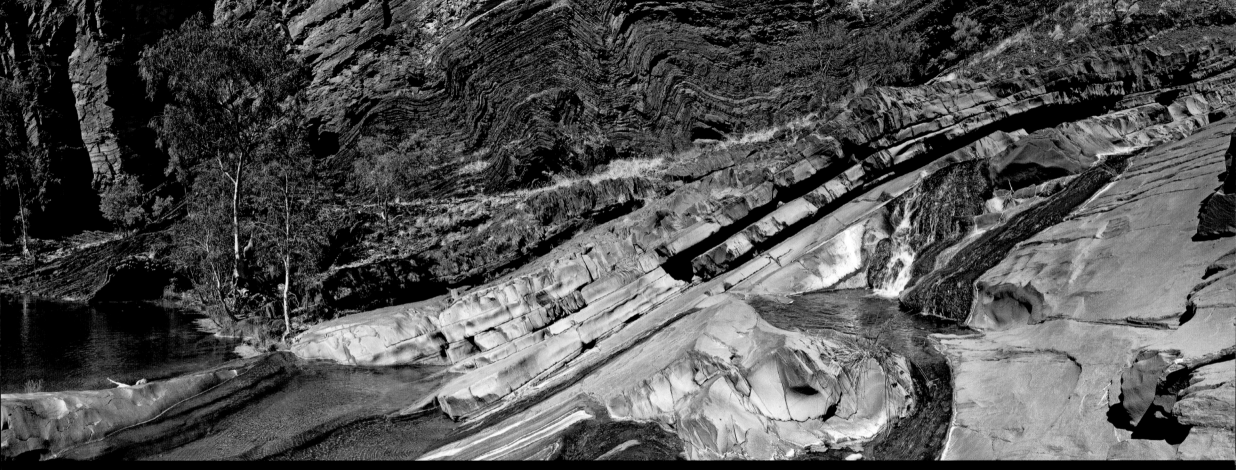

Hamersley Gorge

I do not know anywhere in Western Australia, where the forces of nature show such a range of rock types. The
folds of the Banded Iron Stone are witness to the gigantic forces exerted by continental shifts. On a time scale one
realizes how insignificant our own life span is related to the time it took to fold these multi-layered rocks.

Known as the 'Spar Pool' at Hamersley Gorge, the various metallic colours shine even when the sun is setting.

Fortescue Falls in Dale Gorge

Hamersley Gorge

Fern Pool in Dale Gorge - Dale Gorge is particularly significant to the Banyjima, Kurrama and Yinhawangka people, particularly Circular Pool and Fern Pool.

Waters drips through the porous cracks at Circular Pool watering the many ferns

➤ *Following page*
Reflections on the rock stairways in Kalamina Gorge.
This is one of the easier gorges to walk through.

Kalamina Gorge

The most photographed pool in the Karijini National Park known as Kermit's Pool

The entrance to the narrow gorge that leads to Kermit's Pool looks pretty innocuous, then suddenly you turn the corner and find yourself with boots on one rock face and hands on the other working your way with tripod and camera strapped to your back. Suddenly bells start ringing in your head "Ah, I now know why they call it Spider Walk". You make your way along the narrow gorge with water running between your legs and then you enter one of the most impressive small grottos known as Kermit's Pool. You can make your way to the edge of another waterfall, then look down on the multi coloured steps of the banded ironstone. They shine in the half light, as the water cascades over them. It is a magical location.

Like marbles scattered over the floor, these rock boulders litter the valley adjacent to Python Pool east of Roebourne.

Python Pool is a permanent water hole in Millstream-Chichester National Park

The hills near Comet Mine south of Marble Bar

The jasper bar is just south of the town of Marble Bar. It is part of the Marble Bar greenstone belt consisting of volcanic and sedimentary rocks. Here is a very hard band of jasper chert that holds the water back, creating Chinaman's Pool. Water will not pass over the bar until decent rains fall. For many years the jasper chert bar was considered to be the metamorphic rock, banded marble.

Hills near Taylor's Creek south of Marble Bar

Sunset through the Migum Gum, Hamersley Range.

Mesa's on the Skull Springs Road on the way to Running Waters east of Nullagine

Rolling hills on the Skull Springs Road near Hay's Spring, 60 km east of Nullagine.

Sun filters through the Spinifex at the campsite near Skull Springs

The road in to Carawine Gorge

The abundant late summer rains turn the burnt brown spinifex into
a vibrant green near High Table Hill south east of Roebourne

KIMBERLEY

There is something very special about the Kimberley. For me it is not just the beautiful gorges and rock pools, but the wonderful station owners I know and the characters I meet every time I go there. I also travel on 4WD tracks that few people use and that adds another dimension for me, of peace and spiritual connection with an ancient land. It is a land of permanent water holes, even if the year has experienced drought the big pools will hold water into the next year. The summers can be oppressive but when the 'wet' has set in, its not so bad but it takes two to three weeks on average for people from the south to adapt. The winters are glorious, but that does not last long as there are only about three to four months of moderate weather. If you are planning to visit, a 4WD certainly helps or if not, see the country with a reputable tour operator, someone who has been doing it for a few years. Our photographic journey starts in Broome, a cosmopolitan town, once a sleepy place when I first knew it many years ago. Now a very active tourist destination, but that does not detract from the beautiful sandy beaches and the character of China Town. From there we travel up into the Dampier Peninsula, visiting two communities one at Beagle Bay and one at Lombadina. Both have churches of totally different styles. At the tip of the peninsula is Cape Leveque with more beautiful beaches and a lovely atmosphere. Travelling east of Derby we enter what for me is the true Kimberley, where the mountain ranges start to appear. This is a land of beautiful gorges and rolling hills with pandanus lined creeks and crystal clear waters. The Gibb River Road is now a busy place in the winter months but you can turn off into several destinations and explore those stations like Mornington, Mt Elizabeth, Home Valley or Drysdale River. Around Kununurra there is so much to see and do. Fly over Lake Argyle, take a boat trip along the Ord River, see hundreds of waterbirds on Parry's Lagoon. So much here. Finally our journey looks at the unique colours and textures of the Bungle Bungle, a fitting end to a spectacular region of Western Australia.

Early morning in Purnululu National Park

Some Crested and Lesser Crested Tern as well as the ubiquitous Silver Gull sit out the midday sun at high tide, at Roebuck Bay.

Ruddy Turnstone

The terns and gulls are what we call sedentary birds of the region that is they do not migrate and leave these shores. Bird watchers come to Roebuck Bay for the mass migrations of waders of up to 400,000 birds which congregate at Roebuck Bay over a few months before departing. Although not all will leave and we call this 'over wintering'. Many waders leave Australia's shores in April and make some of the most distant migratory journeys. One bird for example, the Ruddy Turnstone flies as far as the northern boundary of the Tundra as close to the Artic Circle as you could possibly get. There, they nest in the few brief summer months of the northern hemisphere, where for a very short period the temperatures may reach 25°C but in winter those areas plummet to –35°C. Hence, little food and freezing conditions that necessitate birds to make incredibly long journeys to warmer climates, in some cases up to 14,000 km. These journeys take their toll on the waders, but they have adapted to these incredible flights with the aid of a built in biological clock that tells them when they will soon be needing to leave their feeding areas and migrate. Over the weeks before they leave, their feeding rate increases and they put on an amazing amount of body weight, up to 80% of their normal body weight. They will need it because when they finish their journey, the waders may lose 30-50% of their body weight. Some make the journeys without stopping to refuel. It is such a complex operation, as there are so many factors that dictate when and how they will leave. The waders will make their way up the Western Australia coast and many will end up in Roebuck Bay or Ninety Mile Beach. Some have stayed here all summer. Over the weeks, they will build up weight and then start calling to one another and begin to flock. When they do leave they may circle almost as if calling the stragglers, "get on with it and get going guys". They will leave often at dusk, so they do not lose precious energies and fuel (fat content) flying in the heat of the day. The waders also have built in sensors that relate to the magnetic forces of the earth and this assists them in their navigation. They fly at an altitude between 1,000 and 5,000 m because the wind currents there are weaker. They still have the capacity to compensate, if strong winds push them away from their natural course while flying. It's simply an amazing feat.

Twilight on Roebuck Bay

Twilight at Cape Leveque on the Dampier Peninsula. The lighthouse can be seen up on the hill.

The sun sets on the northerly beach at Cape Leveque

The smooth yellow sands contrast with the red pindan rocks at Cape Leveque

The same view at sunset with the tide out

One of my favourite churches in Western Australia at the community in Lombadina on the Dampier Peninsular. No spires here, no gabled stone windows, no vaulted ceilings, just an unpretentious Aussie tin roof and veranda and two simple rows of pews leading to a yellow draped alter.

Beagle Bay

The surveyor J.C. Wickham, who surveyed much of the west Kimberley coastline named Beagle Bay in 1838 after the vessel HMS Beagle. Catholic Lord Bishop Gibney of Perth wished for a mission to be established in the Kimberley under the guidance of the Trappist Fathers from France. It was Dom Ambrose who painstakingly worked on developing the translations of the bible into the local indigenous language Nyul Nyul. In 1901 the German Palontine brothers took over possession of the mission. Then Irish nuns came under the order of Sisters of St John of God in 1907 They taught at the Sacred Heart School. In the initial stages they had 44 girls and 40 boys attending the school. The nuns continued teaching until the mission closed down in the mid 1970's. The Beagle Bay Community from then on became the controlling body for the community but they requested that the Church still be involved in teaching as well as having priests at the church. There are still priests there today. The Church above was built with 60,000 bricks and the local indigenous people assisted by collecting thousands of shells that were used to decorate parts of the church. I remember meeting one of the oldest indigenous men in the Kimberley at Beagle Bay, Rudolph Newman in 2001. He was over 100 then and totally blind but his memory was very sharp. I also spent time with Daniel O'Donovan who had chosen to be a 'Hermit' in the true biblical sense renouncing all luxuries and he certainly did in 2001, for he lived in a small tin shed. Daniel can be seen above in his brilliant red robes. He no longer lives in the small tin shed, but has been given one of the very old original homes of Beagle Bay, It was a real pleasure to see him again after 10 years had passed.

There is a long circular band of limestone which skirts around the base of the Kimberley from off the Dampier Peninsular coast south through Windjana Gorge then across to Geike Gorge and here near Ngumban Cliff between Fitzroy Crossing and Halls Creek. The reef then resurfaces again near Wyndham in the Bonaparte Basin, finding its way back into the ocean. It is known as the Devonian Barrier Reef, a far older reef than the Barrier Reef of Queensland. The reef developed from the compression of millions of years of lime-secreting organisms and shells. Tunnel Creek, Windjanna Gorge and Geikie Gorge are the best places to appreciate the weather sharp landscape of this massive barrier reef.

Windjana Gorge

Windjana Gorge

The Lennard River cuts its way through the 300 million year old limestone Devonian Reef of the Napier Range. At Windjana Gorge the reef is considered to be one of the finest preserved examples of ancient reef systems in the world. There are numerous examples of marine fossils set in the 100 m high walls of the gorge. Winjana is also noted for the exploits of the young Banuba man Jandamarra. This well known story has been written into plays and made into film documentaries. Jandamarra was born around 1873. He was a proficient hunter and the Banuba people think of him as a 'Jalgangurru' a person with extra spiritual powers. Stories have been passed on through the generations at Fitzroy Crossing and other areas. After his early years with his people he entered the world of the Europeans working with William Lukin of Lennard River Station and later with Henry Bostock of Lillimooloora Station. He became a top marksman, stockman and shearer. The Whites named him 'Pigeon' as he was so flight of foot. Later he

rejoined his people to learn more of the Banuba law. In 1890, he was caught with Ellemarra, an older lawman for spearing sheep near Windjana Gorge. Ellemarra had been imprisoned before at Roebourne Prison some 1000 kms from Windjana and had escaped and made it back to his country and was fully aware of the powers of the European. Jandamarra was imprisoned in the Derby Goal but after only six months he was freed as the police realized how skilled he was at all aspects of the bush and they recruited him as a policeman's aid but he returned to his people again. Later he was to return to Lillimooloora Station where he became friends with a Bill Richardson who was soon to join the police force. Richardson soon took Jandamarra on as a police tracker. After some more stock was speared, Jandamarra tracked his people down of which several were senior elders. While in chains, Jandamarra's people talked to him long into the night about what he was doing to his people and the story goes that Ellemarra was in the

group and he would have had a powerful influence on Jandamarra. It must have been a difficult thing being stuck between two worlds and differing moralities. It was too much for Jandamarra and he turned his gun on Richardson. Well, it was on for one and all. The police outpost was raided by the Banuba people including Jandamarra who now took on a lead roll. Weapons and food were taken and they fled into the hills. At the time a big mob of over 500 cattle was being mustered towards Windjana for watering. Led by Fred Edgar in a Wagon and two offsiders on horseback, Frank Bourke and Billy Gibbs with two Aboriginal stockmen, Nuggett and Georgie. In the gorge Bourke, Gibbs and Nugget were speared or shot by Jandamarra's group. Edgar managed to mount a horse and both Edgar and Georgie fled, being pursued by Jandamarra on horseback. Jandamarra's horse tired and Edgar and Georgie made it to Lennard River Station

and word was sent to Derby and Perth of the situation. A party of thirty men from Derby under the command of Sub-inspector Drewery went to Windjana to surprise the Banuba group but Jandamarra was ready. The early morning ambush lasted to midday, no one was killed although Jandamarra was wounded. He and his group hid in the hills at the time. For two years Jandamarra raided stations and stores alike but eventually an indigenous tracker found the tracks of Jandamarra near Tunnel Creek where his blood from a previous wound gave him away and he was eventually shot. His avoidance of authorities and capture makes an amazing story of determination and courage. Sadly many of the Banuba people were killed in reprisals during the years that Jandamarra was on the run.

Why would you take a drive, which on a map reads just 150 kms but in reality, can take you a solid 12 hrs to drive? Why would you drive up some of the most rugged 'jump ups' in Australia and on the way out get stuck in a black soil bog and sleep overnight in a camping rig at a 30-degree angle? Well there are lots of reasons, I have travelled six times on the Munja Track and I would do it all over again, although I will take the mud boards with me next time. One of the reasons is that few people travel it and most of all you travel through some of the most unspoilt country in Australia and the rewards at your destination are the many gorges and pools like the one opposite.

At the gate on the left are two wonderful people, Pat and Peter Lacy. Pat was born in Narrogin and went to work on Peter's station at Mt Elizabeth in April 1969. There they became partners. I have known them for over twenty years and finer people you could not wish to meet. Peter is a man of few words, so you certainly don't do city small talk at Mt Elizabeth, although under that quiet veneer, is a very strong man with an amazing wealth of Kimberley knowledge. The Lacy family's history is a fascinating one. Peter's father Frank was born in New Zealand in 1899 but made the Kimberley his home. They did it tough in those early days, to give you an example

Frank mustered over 1,500 head of cattle and drove them from Spencers Gulf near Wyndam all the way across the most rugged part of the Kimberley to the remote indigenous community of Munja on the Walcott Inlet, imagine that if you know the country. The track that I drive today known as the Munja Track, was opened up by Frank Lacy. Peter's sister and brother-in-law Anne and Rick Jane have kept it open over the last few years. Both Rick and Anne use to run Bush Trek Safaris and like Sammy Lovell, they know this country like the back of their hands.

I was talking to Maisey and Scotty (pic on left) around the breakfast fire one morning about 'country'. Scotty came from Kalumburu and had worked with Frank Lacy for years. He said of Frank "He was the one who grew me up". Maisey, Scotty's partner was born the other side of the Kimberley at Pantijan, north of the old Munja settlement. In her 'dreaming' the Black-headed Python is her totem and none of the family are allowed to kill that snake. They share stories together talking in Ngarinyin, their own language, while I speak to them. While the men were droving, Maisey often baked the bread for the stockmen and also taught all her children what bush tucker to eat. They both have fond memories of Frank Lacy and have a high regard for

Bachsten Gorge looking over the falls to a big pool

A

B

C

D

E

Throughout the Kimberley, particularly in the King Leopold Sandstone country, can be found hundreds of indigenous painting galleries showing wonderful Wandjina and Bradshaw (Gwian Gwian) figures. The first Europeans to describe these paintings like George Grey, Fred Brockman and Joseph Bradshaw talked at length of the many sites they had found on their travels in the Kimberley and how splendid they thought they were.

There are many forms of paintings that can be found in the Kimberley. The most well known are the Wandjina figures shown in *B* and *C*. They are the spirit figures that represent the creation or 'dreaming' time. Indigenous peoples believe that the Wandjinas painted themselves first and that it was the responsibility of the custodians of the stories to repaint them keeping them alive, sadly with the changes in living conditions and the re-settling of people away from their core country has led to most paintings no longer being repainted each season, this I feel, is really sad. Often Wandjinas like those shown here are painted on their sides, often several meters long. They can form the central dominant painting with smaller figures painted around them. These dreaming stories are not just localized, as you will see the same theme depicted in caves two or three hundred kms apart. A typical Bradshaw or Gwian Gwian is shown in photo *A*. Various dates have been placed on Bradshaw paintings but most authorities believe they are the oldest type of painting in the Kimberley as many Wandjinas are painted over them. These figures resemble closely the

costumes of those indigenous Kimberley people that were photographed in the early 20th century. You can see the typical arm and wristbands showing feathers.

Stencil art in *D*, is where the painter blows white ochre from his mouth over his hands. This is a common art form throughout Australia and some say, it is a form of family signature of those responsible for the stories. The grinding hollows you find on the rocks below rock wall galleries are known as 'cupules' shown in photo *E*. They are used for grinding seeds, particularly spinifex seed to make flour. They could also be used to grind coloured ochre to paint with. The King Leopold Sandstone is relatively hard so the depth of these grinding holes gives you an indication of the hundreds, if not thousands of years these hollows have been used by Kimberley people.

It is with respect that these paintings are shown and the locations cannot be given but they are shown so that we all can learn more of their importance and hopefully these wonderful sites may be protected and also some of the young indigenous people can return with elders to 'hold' the stories before they are lost. A few men like Donny Woolagoodja, who I have met, have done so much to keep the Wandjina stories together but it is a big ask, to expect a few men like Donny, to protect such a vast area where precious paintings still exist.

No names for this gorge. The photograph is dedicated to Rick and Anne who know it well.

Quartz rock on Bachsten Creek

The mulla mulla in full bloom on the western side of the Bungle Bungle Range

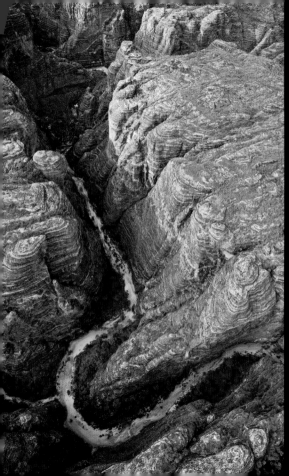

When I first drove into the Bungle Bungle Range in the mid 1980's the track was a rugged 4WD track that took many hours, now it's a lot faster and an easy run. There was almost nobody there in the 80s and now many many people visit this spectacular place. Purnululu National Park is set in the magnificent Bungle Bungle Range. There is nowhere in Australia, in fact the world that has such spectacular beehive domes with such contrasting bands of colour. The Bungle Bungle Range was once an ancient seabed laid down some 300 plus million years ago and over time a sedimentary rock base was laid down from the many rivers that flowed over the region. The massive weight over time compressed the rocks and sand forming sandstone and conglomerate rock you see here. The sands and rocks were slowly uplifted into a mountain range, then with the pressures caused by continental shifts, faults occurred throughout the range and the softer sediments were slowly eroded away. Once cracks developed, the subsequent rains and stone debris cut away huge fissures in the range and over the millions of years the dome formation developed. The erosion process of weathering away the rock is still going on to this day. Many people wonder why there are coloured bands on the domes. Well the scientists and geologists say that with the various periods that sands were deposited differing densities and soil content occurred. Some layers had higher levels of clay. These layers support a microorganism known as cyanobacteria that occurs on the outside, only within a few millimetres but is sufficient enough to slow down the weathering process. The lighter coloured orange bands of sandstone contain less clay so the cyanobacteria is far less prevalent and so wears away much faster. The orange colour occurs from the oxidation of iron in the sandstone. I have taken a few chopper flights over various areas in Australia but few areas compare with the Bungle Bungle Range from the air, it is simply awesome looking down on these domes and to appreciate the forces of nature

Piccaninny Creek, Purnululu National Park.

The Wickham's Grevillea is in full bloom as the morning sun hits the Bungle Bungle Range

I hope you have enjoyed this photographic journey through this vast state of Western Australia.

Acknowledgements

Firstly I wish to thank Sean McKay, the graphic designer and his wife Sally. I found a gem of a designer in Sean making the task of producing this book such a pleasure and his talent certainly shows.

To Anne Ireland who has been so supportive on my journey over the last year to get this book to print and assisting with text alterations and who believed I could do it. To my good friend Pura Mohsenzadeh for double checking the text. To my long term buddy Colin Andrews for checking text. To the many staff I know at DEC (Department of Environment and Conservation) who make the many parks in this state a pleasure to visit, often working under tight budgetary constraints. The quality of information boards and general facilities in general are fantastic. When I first made the rugged journey into the Mitchell Plateaux region in the mid 1980's there were no other people camping there at the time. Now there are over 15,000 people entering this park each year. In just 25 years the pressure on the department through visitor numbers increases day by day but they still manage with the help of good rangers and volunteers to manage these parks so well. To the communities of Papulankutja and Warakurna for letting me enter your country. To the 'Bunbury and Mandurah' convoy on the Munja Track for winching me out of the bog. You were a great team and Anne and I enjoyed the journey out with you.

This book is dedicated to Willy Teo

Over a year ago, I had to give a slide presentation when I was extremely busy and it was all a bit rushed. When I got to the lecture hall, the dear projector would not talk to the screen or to me. A quiet gentleman came up and said to me "Mr Nevill, can I help?" Well being the talented engineer he is, it was fixed in no time at all. After the talk, I asked the organizer who the gentleman was, so I could thank him but alas, he had already gone. I did not forget him and gave him a ring. From that call we have developed an amazing friendship. We share so many similar values in life even though we were born thousands of miles apart. He has stretched the left side of my brain to its very limit, helping me with technical aspects of Lightroom and Photoshop but the thing I value the most is his friendship. May you long remain on the third rung of the ladder as you put it, Willy. I wish you and Louise and your children all the best through the years ahead.

Photograph locations

The numbers featured below relate to the page number and the approximate geographical location of each photograph.

About the author

I have had many occupations in life but my happiest work is what I do now, creating and producing books and hopefully passing information to people that may interest them. Sadly, I do not make the monies I once did but I have never lived for money and the joy I get standing say on a breakaway ridge in the middle of the desert photographing a sunrise or sunset gives me the most intrinsic rewards I could wish for. I will keep doing what I love, until the legs wont take me up to the top of the mountains any more. Until then I do hope the books I produce give pleasure to many.

Other titles by the author

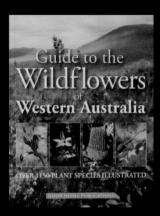

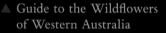

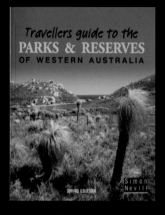

▲ Guide to the Wildflowers of Western Australia

▲ Travellers Guide to the Parks & Reserves of Western Australia

▲ Guide to the Wildlife of the Perth Region

If you have problems obtaining any of these books, please email snpub@bigpond.net.au

▲ Perth and Fremantle Past and Present

▲ Birds of the Greater South West, Western Australia